RAND McNALLY | Schoolhouse

World Atlas

Beginner

Managing Editor
Brett Gover

Cartographic Project Manager
Nina Lusterman

Cartography
Robert Argersinger
Marzee Eckhoff
David Simmons

Photo Credits
p. 4: earth © Photodisc; p. 10: forestry, farming © Photodisc; trade © Getty; herding © Grant Dixon/Lonely Planet Images; p. 12: skiing © Getty; rain forest © Photodisc; olive groves © Oliver Strewe/Lonely Planet Images; farming © Andrew Brownbill/Lonely Planet Images; p. 13: cactus © Photodisc; p. 16: maize © Getty; Vikings, cliff dwellings © Photodisc; p. 17: outer banks © Corbis; Capitol building, mountains, Grand Canyon, Maine, California, Badlands, farms, Statue of Liberty © Photodisc; antique map, ship, flag © Getty; p. 19: bear, wheat field, National University, Statue of Liberty © Photodisc; Aztec symbol © Neil Setchfield/Lonely Planet Images; ship © Corbis; antique map, flag, Panama Canal © Getty; p. 21: giant tortoise © Corbis; rain forest, Machu Picchu, market © Photodisc; Portuguese flag, Spanish flag, South American flags, Buenos Aires © Getty; p. 24: Parthenon, Eiffel Tower, Colosseum, Big Ben, aqueduct, painting © Photodisc; Minoan pots, European town © Corbis; p. 25: Matterhorn, basket maker, train, Columbus © Photodisc; skier, cogs © Getty; antique map, ruin © Corbis; p. 27: Sphinx, pyramids; gorilla © Getty; building © Andrew Burke/Lonely Planet Images; Kush art © Anders Blomqvist/Lonely Planet Images; Egyptian art, antique map, ship, European flags, African flags © Corbis; p. 30: farming, oil refinery, Hong Kong, Himalayas, wheat, Great Wall © Photodisc; China © Chris Mellor/Lonely Planet Images; ruins © Dallas Stribley/Lonely Planet Images; Sumerian ruins © Jane Sweeney/Lonely Planet Images; paper © Getty; p. 31: panda, Taj Mahal, Tokyo, Great Wall © Photodisc; European flags © Corbis; Indian flag © Getty; p. 33: kangaroo, northern Australia, British flag, Australian flag © Getty; Uluru© Richard I'Anson/Lonely Planet Images; Sydney, telescope © Photodisc; Great Barrier Reef, gold © Corbis; p. 35: penguin 1, penguin 2, scientists, Antarctica © Getty; iceberg, science station © Corbis; compass © Photodisc; p. 36: mountain, harbor, coast © Photodisc; p. 37: desert, island, forest, valley © Photodisc; p. 39: ocean, river, city, mountains © Photodisc

Printed in the United States of America.

Rand McNally & Company
Skokie, Illinois 60076-8906

ISBN 528-93463-5

10 9 8 7 6 5 4 3

For information about ordering the *Schoolhouse Beginner World Atlas*, call 1-800-678-RAND (-7263) or visit our website at www.randmcnally.com.

Table of Contents

Maps and Globes

Maps and globes help people learn about the earth.

A **globe** is a model of the earth.

A **map** is a drawing of the earth's surface.

Earth from space

The earth is shaped like a **sphere**, or ball. This picture taken from space shows some of the earth's land and water through clouds.

Did You **Know?**

Water covers about three-fourths of the earth's surface. From space the earth looks blue.

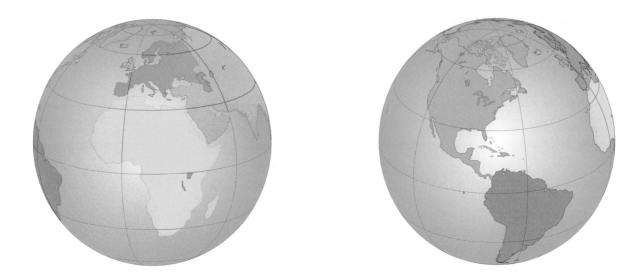

A globe is shaped like the earth. When you turn the globe, you see a different part of the earth.

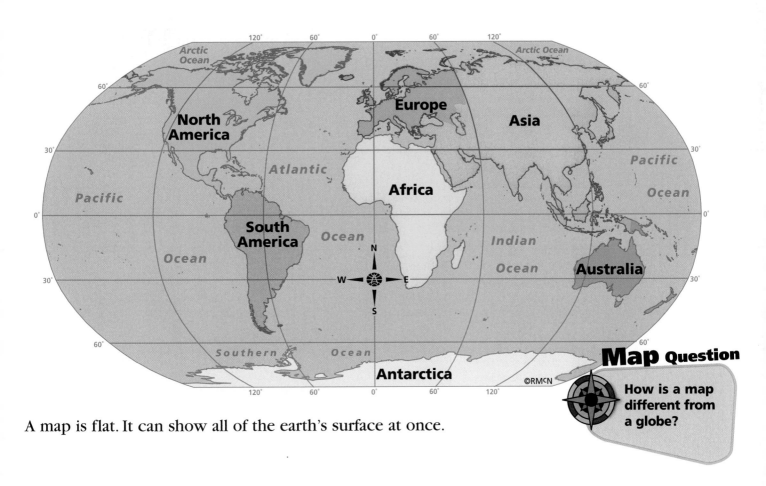

A map is flat. It can show all of the earth's surface at once.

Map Question

How is a map different from a globe?

The World's Land and Water

The world is made up of land and water. **Continents** are the largest bodies of land. **Oceans** are the largest bodies of water.

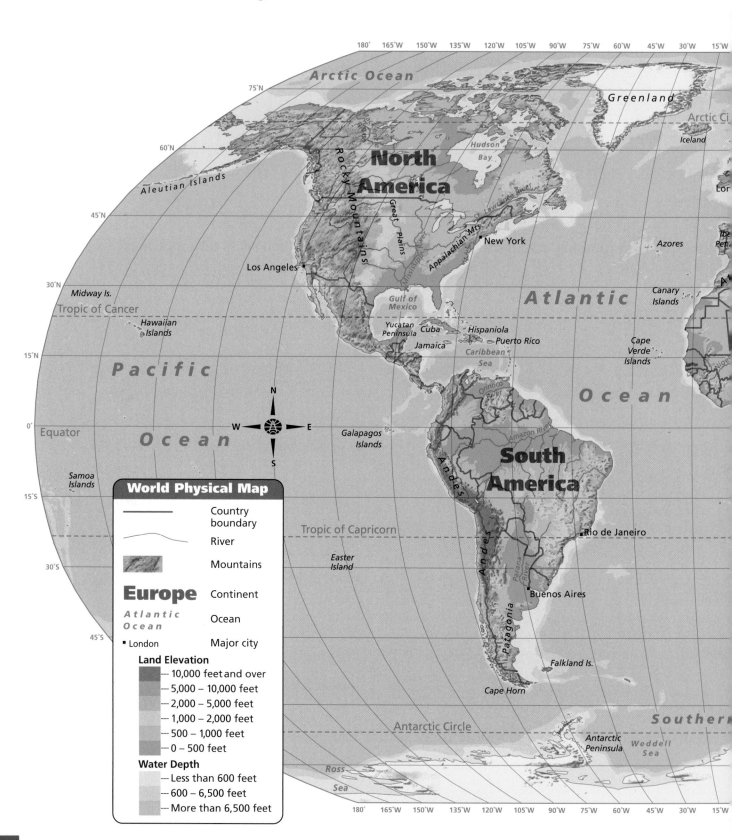

World Physical Map

——	Country boundary
~~	River
	Mountains
Europe	Continent
Atlantic Ocean	Ocean
▪ London	Major city

Land Elevation
- 10,000 feet and over
- 5,000 – 10,000 feet
- 2,000 – 5,000 feet
- 1,000 – 2,000 feet
- 500 – 1,000 feet
- 0 – 500 feet

Water Depth
- Less than 600 feet
- 600 – 6,500 feet
- More than 6,500 feet

15°E 30°E 45°E 60°E 75°E 90°E 105°E 120°E 135°E 150°E 165°E 180°

Arctic Ocean

75°N

Scandinavian Peninsula

Europe

60°N

Siberia

• Moscow

Ural Mts.

Volga River

Ob River

Yenisei River

Lena River

Amur River

Bering Sea

Sea of Okhotsk

Kamchatka Peninsula

45°N

Alps

Balkan Peninsula

Black Sea

Caucasus

Aral Sea

Asia

Altai Mts.

Pamirs

Gobi Desert

Beijing •

Huang River

Sea of Japan

Mediterranean Sea

Zagros Mts.

Plateau of Tibet

Himalayas

Yangtze River

East China Sea

Pacific

30°N

Cairo •

Nile River

Red Sea

Arabian Peninsula

Bombay •

Ganges River

Deccan Plateau

Taiwan

Tropic of Cancer

ra Desert

ahel

Arabian Sea

Sri Lanka

South China Sea

Luzon

Guam •

Ocean

15°N

Africa

Ethiopian Plateau

Mindanao

Congo River

Great Rift Valley

Malay Peninsula

Borneo

Celebes

New Guinea

Solomon Islands

Equator

0°

Sumatra

Java

Indian

Zambezi River

Madagascar

Coral Sea

15°S

Kalahari Desert

Great Sandy Desert

Australia

Darling River

Great Dividing Range

Tropic of Capricorn

Ocean

30°S

Cape of Good Hope

Sydney •

North Island

Tasmania

South Island

45°S

| 0 | 1000 | 2000 | 3000 Miles |

Ocean

Antarctic Circle

75°S

Antarctica

Copyright by Rand McNally & Co.
Made in U.S.A.
N-JRC10000-A1- -3-3-3

15°E 30°E 45°E 60°E 75°E 90°E 105°E 120°E 135°E 150°E 165°E 180°

Map Question

Which ocean is between the continents of North America and Europe?

7

The World's Countries

The world's continents are divided into **countries**.
A **country boundary** shows where a country begins and ends.

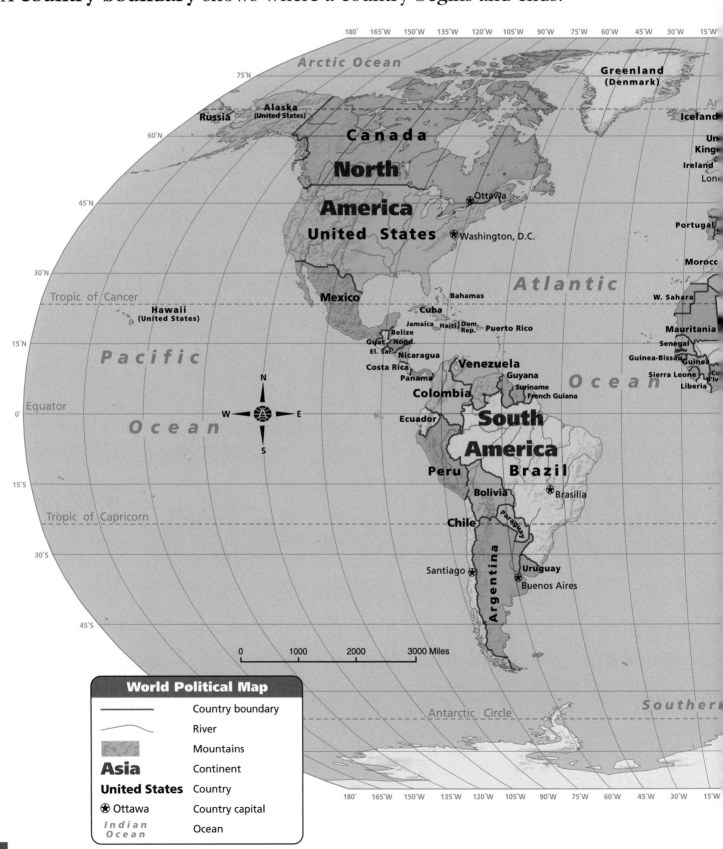

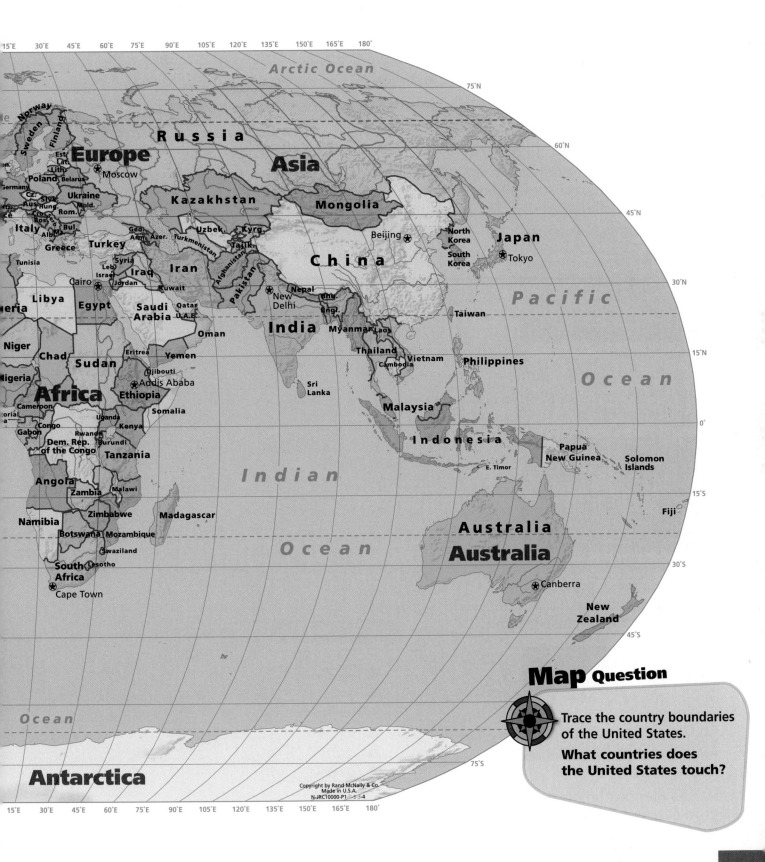

Map Question

Trace the country boundaries of the United States.

What countries does the United States touch?

World Land Use

People use the world's land in different ways. Many people in cities earn a living by **manufacturing**, or making goods.

Forestry in North America

Trees from North America's forests provide such things as lumber for building houses and pulp for making paper.

Trade in Europe

Europe has many busy ports where ships load and unload goods from around the world.

Herding in South America

Herders in some parts of South America raise llamas. These animals provide wool and transportation.

Farming in Asia

Rice is the most important crop grown in Asia. It can be grown on flat land or even on steep hillsides.

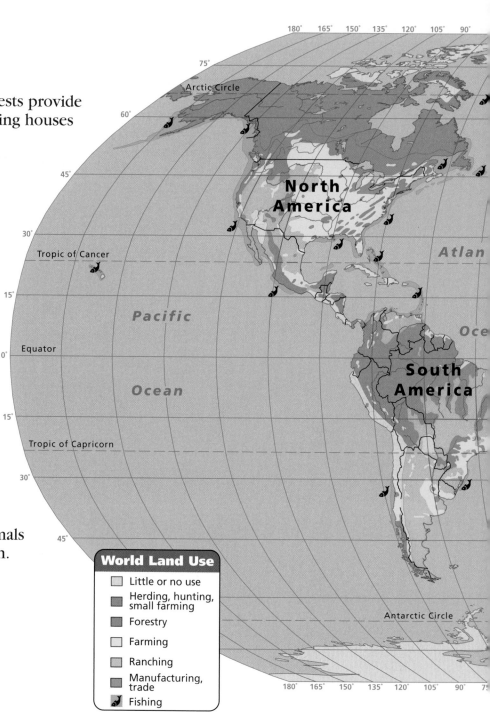

North America

South America

Pacific

Ocean

Atlan

Oce

Arctic Circle

Tropic of Cancer

Equator

Tropic of Capricorn

Antarctic Circle

World Land Use

- Little or no use
- Herding, hunting, small farming
- Forestry
- Farming
- Ranching
- Manufacturing, trade
- Fishing

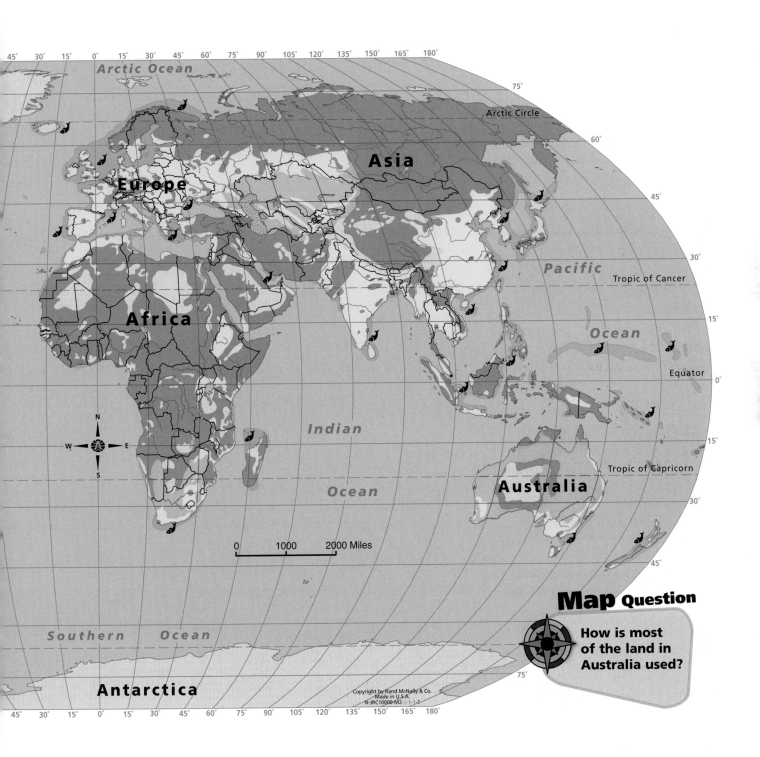

Map Question

How is most of the land in Australia used?

World Climate

Climate is how hot or cold, wet or dry a place is.
Some places have a climate that changes with the seasons.

Cross-country skiing in Canada

Parts of Canada have long, cold winters and short, cool summers.

Rain forest in Brazil

Rain forests receive more than 80 inches of rain a year. Many of the world's rain forests are near the equator.

Olive groves in Spain

Parts of Spain have hot, dry summers and rainy winters.

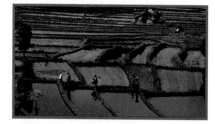

Farming in Indonesia

Rice grows well in places that are hot and rainy all year.

World Climate Map

- ■ Warmest climates
- ■ Coldest climates
- ■ Deserts
- ■ Rain forests
- ■ Climates change with the seasons

Did You Know?

A saguaro is a giant cactus that grows in very dry places in North America. It may grow to be 60 feet tall.

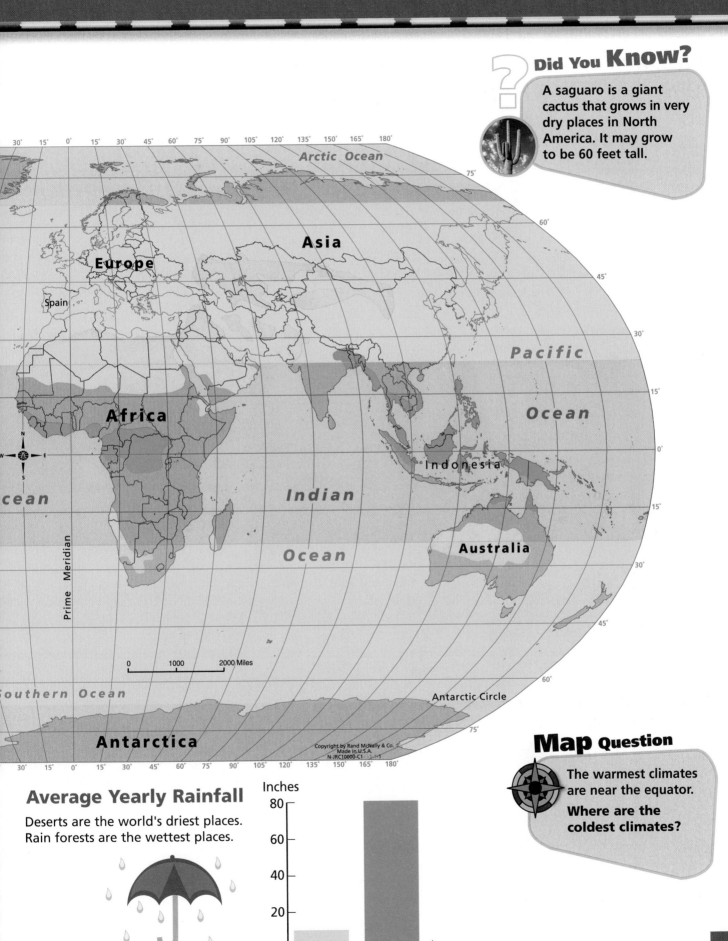

30° 15° 0° 15° 30° 45° 60° 75° 90° 105° 120° 135° 150° 165° 180°

Arctic Ocean

75°

60°

Asia

Europe

45°

Spain

30°

Pacific

15°

Africa

Ocean

0°

W—E N S

Indonesia

Indian

15°

cean

Australia

Ocean

30°

Prime Meridian

0   1000   2000 Miles

60°

Southern Ocean

Antarctic Circle

75°

Antarctica

Copyright by Rand McNally & Co.
Made in U.S.A.
N-JRC10000-C1   1

30° 15° 0° 15° 30° 45° 60° 75° 90° 105° 120° 135° 150° 165° 180°

Average Yearly Rainfall

Deserts are the world's driest places. Rain forests are the wettest places.

Inches

80

60

40

20

0

Desert   Rain forest

Map Question

The warmest climates are near the equator.

Where are the coldest climates?

13

United States

The **United States** is made up of fifty states. Each state has a **state capital**, which is a city where state government leaders work.

Map Question

What city is the capital of your state?

95° 90° 85° 80° 75° 70° 65°

a d a

45°

Minnesota
argo

Lake Superior

Great Lakes

New Hampshire

Vermont

★ Augusta

Maine

★ Portland

Montpelier ★

★ Concord

Michigan

St. Paul ★
Minneapolis ★

Wisconsin
Green Bay ■

Lake Michigan

Lake Huron

Lake Ontario

40°

Buffalo ■

New York

Mass. ★ Boston
Albany ★ Cape Cod
Hartford ★ Providence
Conn. **R.I.**

ux Falls
Sioux City ■

Milwaukee ■
Madison ★
Rockford ■

Grand Rapids ■
★ Lansing
Detroit ■

Lake Erie

Cleveland ■

Pennsylvania

Long Island
New York ■

aha
Iowa ■ Cedar
Rapids
Des Moines ■

Chicago ■
Peoria ■

Ohio

Columbus

Pittsburgh ■ Harrisburg ★

★ Trenton

Philadelphia ■

New Jersey

oln

Illinois
Springfield ★

Indiana
Indianapolis ★

Cincinnati ■

West Virginia

Baltimore ■ ★ Dover
Annapolis ★ **Delaware**
⊛ Washington D.C.

eka ★
Kansas ■
City

St. Louis ■

Louisville ■

★ Frankfort

Charleston ★

Richmond ★

Maryland

35°

Jefferson
City ★

Evansville ■ Ohio River

Kentucky

Virginia

★ Norfolk ■

Atlantic Ocean

hita

Missouri

Nashville ★

Winston-Salem ★
Raleigh ★

Cape Hatteras

Tulsa ■

River

Tennessee

North Carolina

Memphis ■ Tennessee River

Charlotte ■

lahoma
Fort Smith ■
Arkansas

Little
Rock ★

South Carolina
★ Columbia

Birmingham ■

★ Atlanta

Charleston ■

allas
Shreveport ■

Mississippi

Alabama

Columbus ■

Georgia

Montgomery ★

Jackson ★

Louisiana

Baton
Rouge ★

Jacksonville ■

Tallahassee ★

Houston ■

New
Orleans ■

Trinity River

N
W ✦ E
S

Orlando ■

Florida

Cape Canaveral

Gulf of Mexico

Tampa ■

The
Everglades

Miami ■

Bahamas

0 100 200 300 400 Miles

Florida Keys

Appalachian Mountains

Mississippi River
Missouri River
Illinois River

United States	
▬▬▬	Country boundary
———	State boundary
〰	River
Canada	Country
Ohio	State
⊛ Washington D.C.	Country capital
★ Denver	State capital
■ Dallas	City
Atlantic Ocean	Ocean
〰〰	Swamp

95° 90° 85° 80° 75°

United States Regions

The United States can be divided into regions in many different ways. This map shows one way.

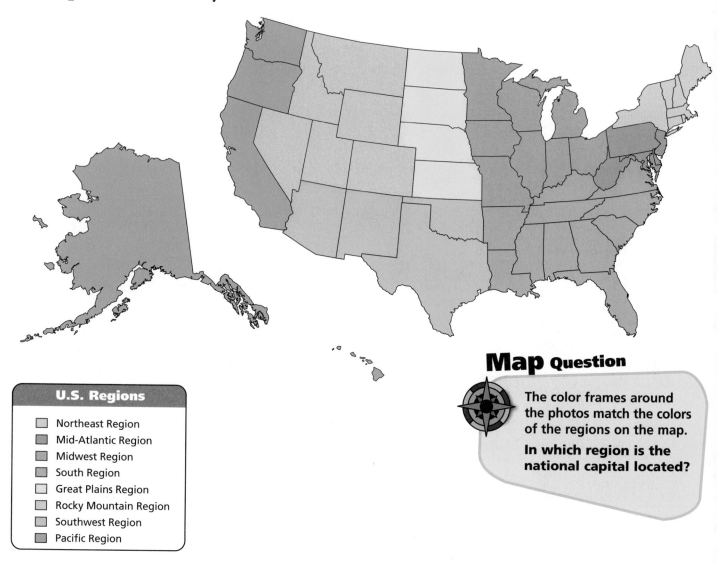

U.S. Regions

- Northeast Region
- Mid-Atlantic Region
- Midwest Region
- South Region
- Great Plains Region
- Rocky Mountain Region
- Southwest Region
- Pacific Region

Map Question

The color frames around the photos match the colors of the regions on the map.

In which region is the national capital located?

The United States through History

About 1,200 years ago

The Hohokam farmed in the desert Southwest.

About 800 years ago

The Anasazi built cliff dwellings in the Southwest.

| 900 A.D. | 1000 A.D. | 1100 | 1200 | 1300 | 1400 |

About 1,000 years ago

Vikings from Greenland explored the northeast coast of North America.

The Outer Banks of North Carolina

The United States Capitol building in Washington, D.C.

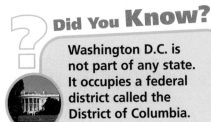

Did You Know?

Washington D.C. is not part of any state. It occupies a federal district called the District of Columbia.

Mountains in Colorado

The Grand Canyon in Arizona

Fall in Maine

The coast of California

Badlands in South Dakota

Farms in Wisconsin

About 500 years ago

Spanish explorers traveled through the south and southwestern parts of what is now the United States.

A little more than 200 years ago

The colonies won freedom from Great Britain, and the United States became a nation.

1500 ▶ 1600 ▶ 1700 ▶ 1800 ▶ 1900 ▶ 2000

About 400 years ago

English settlers started colonies along the Atlantic Coast.
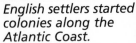

About 100 years ago

Millions of European immigrants settled in the United States.

North America

North America is the continent where we live. The United States is the second-largest country in North America.

Map Question

North America's largest country is a little larger than the United States.

What country is it?

ASIA

Arctic Ocean

Bering Strait

Bering Sea

Greenland (Denmark)

Arctic Circle

Alaska (United States)

▲ Mt. McKinley 20,320 ft.

Anchorage ■

Godthab ✪

Pacific Ocean

Hudson Bay

C a n a d a

Edmonton ■

Vancouver ■

Calgary ■

Seattle ■

Rocky Mountains

Winnipeg ■

Great Plains

Missouri River

St. Lawrence River

Québec ■

Montréal ■

Ottawa ✪

Toronto ■

Great Lakes

San Francisco ■

Denver ■

Colorado River

Chicago ■

Detroit ■

New York ■

Appalachian Mts.

Los Angeles ■

San Diego ■

Phoenix ■

United States

Mississippi River

Ohio River

Washington D.C. ✪

Dallas ■

Atlanta ■

Atlantic Ocean

Rio Grande

Houston ■

Gulf of Mexico

Miami ■

Bahamas

Dominican Republic

Tropic of Cancer

Monterrey ■

Mexico

Havana ✪ Cuba

Jamaica

Haiti

Puerto Rico (United States)

Guadalajara ■

Mexico City ✪

Belize

Honduras

Caribbean Sea

Guatemala

El Salvador

Nicaragua

Costa Rica

Panama

SOUTH AMERICA

Equator

North America

———	Country boundary
⌒	River
▲	Highest point
Canada	Country
✪ Havana	Country capital
■ Montréal	City
Pacific Ocean	Ocean

N
W E
S

0 200 400 600 800 1000 Miles

120°   105°   90°   75°

165° 75° 75° 0°
60° 15°
180° 60°
165° 30°
45°
45°
30° 60°
30°
15°
0° 0°

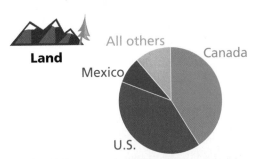

Did You **Know?**

Grizzly bears are found mostly in Alaska and western Canada.

Comparing Countries in North America

The United States and Canada are almost the same size. The United States has more people than any other country in North America.

Land
All others
Canada
Mexico
U.S.

People
All others
Canada
Mexico
U.S.

Wheat field on the Great Plains

The Great Plains region stretches through Canada and the United States. Wheat is the major crop.

National University in Mexico City

Mexico City is a center of art and learning. This school is the largest university in Mexico.

The Statue of Liberty in New York Harbor

The Statue of Liberty welcomes people from other countries who come to live in the United States.

North America through History

About 700 years ago

The Aztecs built an empire in Mexico.

About 400 years ago

Europeans started colonies in North America.

About 100 years ago

The Panama Canal linked the Atlantic and Pacific Oceans.

| 1300 | 1400 | 1500 | 1600 | 1700 | 1800 | 1900 | 2000 |

About 500 years ago
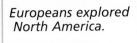
Europeans explored North America.

About 200 years ago
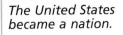
The United States became a nation.

South America

South America has thirteen mainland countries.
All but two of them are located along a coast.

Map Legend — **South America**
- Country boundary
- River
- ▲ Highest point
- **Bolivia** Country
- ✪ Lima Country capital
- ■ São Paulo City
- *Atlantic Ocean* Ocean

0 200 400 600 800 1000 Miles

Copyright by Rand McNally & Co.
Made in U.S.A.
N-JRC40000-P1

Map Question

Which two South American countries are not along a coast?

? Did You **Know?**

The giant tortoises of the Galapagos Islands can live for more than 140 years.

That's a Lot of Coffee!

Brazil and Colombia produce more coffee beans than any other countries in the world.

Brazil 🫘🫘🫘🫘🫘🫘🫘🫘🫘🫘🫘🫘🫘🫘🫘🫘🫘🫘🫘🫘🫘🫘🫘🫘🫘

Colombia 🫘🫘🫘🫘🫘🫘🫘🫘🫘🫘

Indonesia 🫘🫘🫘🫘🫘

Vietnam 🫘🫘🫘🫘

Each 🫘 = 100,000 tons of coffee beans

Amazon rain forest in Brazil

The world's largest tropical rain forest covers most of northern South America.

Machu Picchu in Peru

The stone ruins of this ancient Inca city are high in the Andes Mountains.

Outdoor market in Ecuador

Indians from villages in the Andes gather to buy and sell goods.

South America through History

About 600 years ago

The Inca ruled lands along the west coast of South America.

About 400 years ago

Spain ruled much of South America.

About 100 years ago

One million people lived in Buenos Aires, Argentina.

1400 ▶ 1500 ▶ 1600 ▶ 1700 ▶ 1800 ▶ 1900 ▶ 2000

About 500 years ago

Portugal claimed Brazil.

About 200 years ago

South American countries won their freedom from European rulers.

21

Europe

Europe is a small continent, but it has many people.
It has some of the world's most famous cities.

45°   60°   75°
                                    60°

Map Question

Moscow is Europe's largest city.

In what country is it located?

75°

R u s s i a

Ural Mountains

Perm ■

A s i a

Volga River

Kama River

45°

❋ Moscow

K a z a k h s t a n

Volgograd ■

Volga River

Kiev

U k r a i n e

Caspian Sea

60°

Caucasus

▲ Mt. Elbrus
18,510 ft.

Azerbaijan

Black Sea

Istanbul

r k e y

A s i a

Europe	
————	Country boundary
〰️	River
▲	Highest point
Spain	Country
❋ Paris	Country capital
■ Munich	City
Atlantic Ocean	Ocean

30°

0   100   200   300   400   500 Miles

S e a

30°   45°

23

The Parthenon in Athens, Greece

This ancient temple was built by the Greeks to honor the goddess Athena.

The Eiffel Tower in Paris, France

The Eiffel Tower is a popular place for tourists to visit. They can go to the top of the 984-foot tower for a view of Paris.

The Colosseum in Rome, Italy

This large outdoor amphitheater was built by the Romans almost 2,000 years ago.

Tower of Big Ben in London, England

Big Ben is a famous bell in the clock tower of the Houses of Parliament in London.

Europe through History

About 5,000 years ago

Minoan culture began on the island of Crete.

About 2,000 years ago

The Roman Empire ruled a huge area around the Mediterranean Sea.

About 700 years ago

The Renaissance brought new interest in art and science.

| 3000 B.C. | 2000 B.C. | 1000 B.C. | 1000 A.D. | 1100 | 1200 | 1300 |

About 4,500 years ago

Greek civilization began.

About 1,000 years ago

Towns began to grow in Europe.

The Matterhorn is one of the most famous mountains in the world.

This graph compares the populations of five of Europe's largest cities.

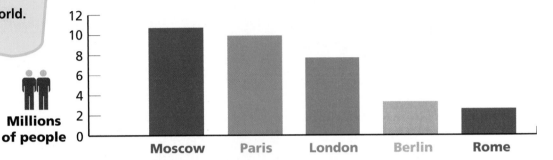

Millions of people

Moscow	Paris	London	Berlin	Rome

Basketmaker in Croatia

Europe has many factories, but some workers make goods by hand.

High-speed train in France

Express trains carry passengers to major cities throughout Europe.

Skiing in the Alps

Winter sports are popular in many parts of Europe.

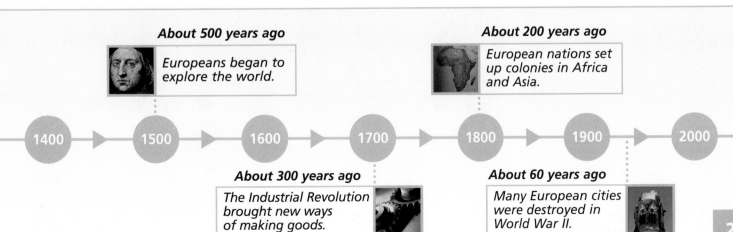

About 500 years ago

Europeans began to explore the world.

About 200 years ago

European nations set up colonies in Africa and Asia.

1400   1500   1600   1700   1800   1900   2000

About 300 years ago

The Industrial Revolution brought new ways of making goods.

About 60 years ago

Many European cities were destroyed in World War II.

Africa

Africa has both rain forests and deserts. The Sahara is the largest desert in the world. It covers most of the northern part of the continent.

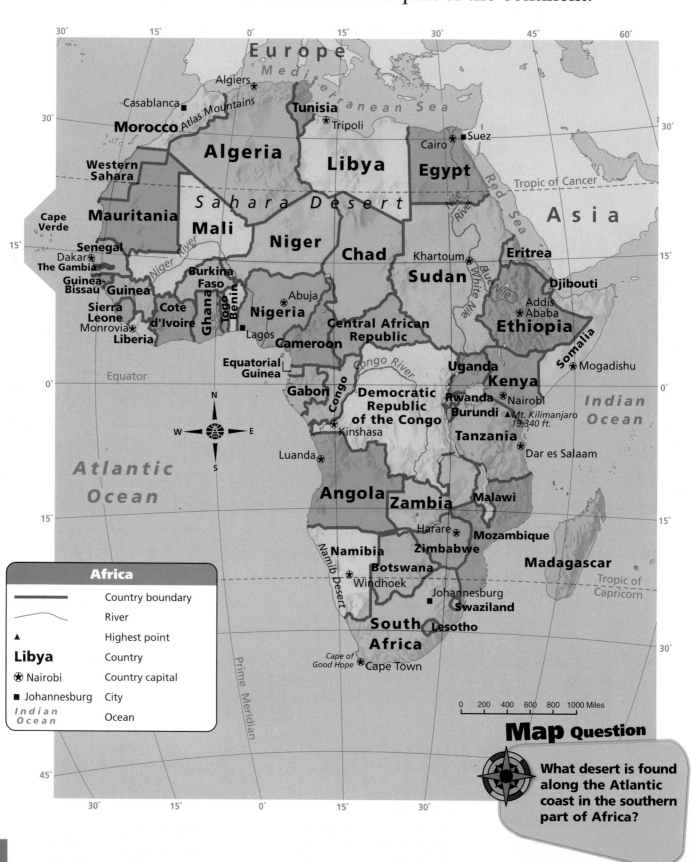

Africa

———	Country boundary
⌒	River
▲	Highest point
Libya	Country
✪ Nairobi	Country capital
■ Johannesburg	City
Indian Ocean	Ocean

Map Question

What desert is found along the Atlantic coast in the southern part of Africa?

The Longest River on Each Continent

The Nile River in Africa is the longest river in the world.

Nile (Africa)		4,145 miles
Amazon (South America)		4,000 miles
Yangtze (Asia)		3,900 miles
Mississippi-Missouri (North America)		3,740 miles
Murray-Darling (Australia)		2,330 miles
Volga (Europe)		2,194 miles

Ancient statues in Egypt

These giant statues were carved thousands of years ago. They were part of a temple honoring an Egyptian king.

Lowland gorilla in central Africa

Lowland gorillas live in rain forests near the equator.

Modern buildings in Johannesburg, South Africa

Johannesburg is the largest city in South Africa. It is one of Africa's most important trade centers.

Africa Through History

About 5,100 years ago

Egypt became a great kingdom.

About 600 years ago

Powerful kingdoms began in central and southern Africa.

About 100 years ago

European countries ruled most of Africa.

 3000 B.C. → 1000 B.C. → 1400 A.D. → 1600 → 1800 → 2000

About 4,000 years ago

The kingdom of Kush became a center of art, learning, and trade.

About 500 years ago

Portuguese explorers sailed around Africa to India.

About 50 years ago

African countries began to win freedom from European rule.

27

Asia

Asia is the largest continent. It has more land and more people than any other continent.

Map labels:

Arctic Ocean

Europe

Moscow

Russia

Arctic Circle

Ural Mountains

Ob River

Sib...

Omsk

Novosibirsk

Astana

Kazakhstan

Mongoli...

Ankara

Turkey

Georgia

Armenia

Azerbaijan

Cyprus

Lebanon

Israel

Syria

Jerusalem

Egypt

Jordan

Iraq

Baghdad

Tehran

Kuwait

Iran

Uzbekistan

Turkmenistan

Kyrgyzstan

Tajikistan

Ch i...

Kabul

Afghanistan

Islamabad

Indus River

Himalayas

Jiddah

Riyadh

Bahrain

Qatar

U.A.E.

Saudi Arabia

Muscat

Sanaa

Yemen

Oman

Pakistan

Karachi

New Delhi

Ganges River

Nepal

Mt. Everest 29,028 ft.

Bhutan

Bangladesh

Ayeyarwady River

India

Calcutta

Bombay

Myanmar (Burma)

Rangoon

Bangalore

Madras

Bay of Bengal

Bangko...

Sri Lanka

Arabian Sea

Red Sea

Mediterranean Sea

Black Sea

Caspian Sea

Tigris River

Euphrates River

Tropic of Cancer

Africa

Equator

Indian Ocean

N W E S

Asia

———	Country boundary
∿	River
▲	Highest point
China	Country
✪ Tehran	Country capital
■ Bombay	City
Pacific Ocean	Ocean

0 200 400 600 800 1000 Miles

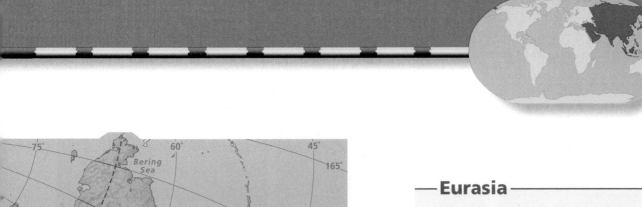

Eurasia

The continents of Europe and Asia form one large body of land called Eurasia.

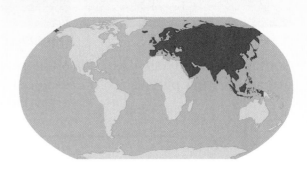

Map Question

The world's largest country covers much of Asia and Europe.

What country is it?

29

Asia

Farming in Indonesia

Some farmers in Asia use animals to pull plows.

Transportation in China

Many people use bicycles to get around in China's crowded cities.

Oil refinery in Southwest Asia

Much of the world's oil comes from countries in Southwest Asia.

Hong Kong Harbor

Hong Kong is one of the most important port cities in Asia.

The Himalayas in Nepal

The Himalayas are the highest mountains in the world. Their name means "House of Snow."

Ancient ruins in Turkey

Turkey is the westernmost country in Asia.

Asia through History

About 11,000 years ago

People began farming in Southwest Asia.

About 2,200 years ago

China began building the Great Wall.

9000 B.C.	7000 B.C.	5000 B.C.	3000 B.C	1000 B.C	1000 A.D.

About 5,500 years ago

Civilization began between the Tigris and Euphrates Rivers.

About 1,900 years ago

The Chinese invented paper.

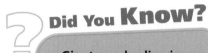
World Population

Asia has more people than all the other continents added together.

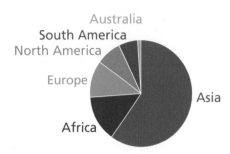

Australia
South America
North America
Europe
Asia
Africa

The Taj Mahal in India

An Indian ruler built the Taj Mahal in memory of his wife. The beautiful building is made of white marble.

Skyscrapers in Tokyo, Japan

Tokyo is the capital of Japan. It is the largest city in the world.

The Great Wall of China

The Chinese built the Great Wall to protect their country. It is about 25 feet high and 4,600 miles long.

About 400 years ago

The Taj Mahal was built in India.

About 50 years ago

India and other Asian nations won freedom.

| 1200 | 1400 | 1600 | 1800 | 2000 |

About 200 years ago

European nations controlled parts of Asia.

Australia

Australia is both a continent and a country. It is the world's smallest continent, but it is the sixth-largest country.

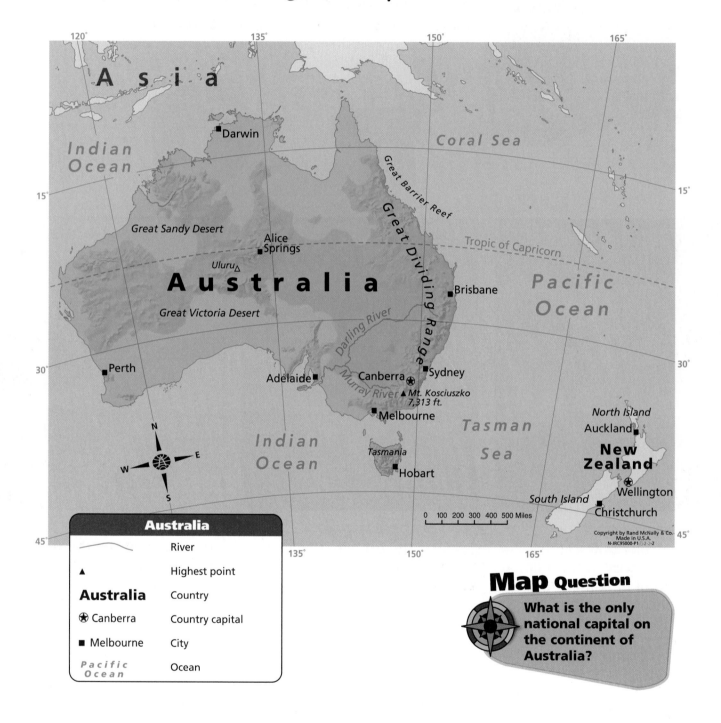

Australia

⌒ River	River
▲	Highest point
Australia	Country
✪ Canberra	Country capital
■ Melbourne	City
Pacific Ocean	Ocean

Map Question

What is the only national capital on the continent of Australia?

Did You **Know?**

A kangaroo can hop as fast as 30 miles per hour. It can jump six feet high.

Leading Sheep-Raising Countries

Australia is the world's leading producer of sheep and wool.

Australia	🐑🐑🐑🐑🐑🐑🐑🐑🐑🐑🐑🐑🐑🐑🐑🐑🐑🐑
China	🐑🐑🐑🐑🐑🐑🐑🐑🐑🐑🐑🐑🐑🐑
New Zealand	🐑🐑🐑🐑🐑
Iran	🐑🐑🐑🐑
India	🐑🐑🐑🐑

Each 🐑 = 10 million sheep

Uluru, near Alice Springs

Uluru is also called Ayers Rock. It has many caves with paintings made by people who lived there long ago.

Sydney Opera House and skyline

Sydney is the largest city in Australia. The Sydney Opera House is the city's most famous landmark.

The Great Barrier Reef

Divers can see many kinds of fish and coral along the Great Barrier Reef. The reef stretches for more than 1,200 miles along the northeast coast of Australia.

Australia Through History

About 600 years ago

Chinese settlers arrived in northern Australia.

About 200 years ago
Great Britain began to claim land in Australia.

About 100 years ago

Australia became a nation.

| 1400 | ▶ | 1500 | ▶ | 1600 | ▶ | 1700 | ▶ | 1800 | ▶ | 1900 | ▶ | 2000 |

About 400 years ago
Dutch sailors explored the coasts of Australia.

About 150 years ago
Gold was discovered in Australia.

Antarctica

Antarctica is the coldest continent. A thick layer of ice and snow covers most of the land.

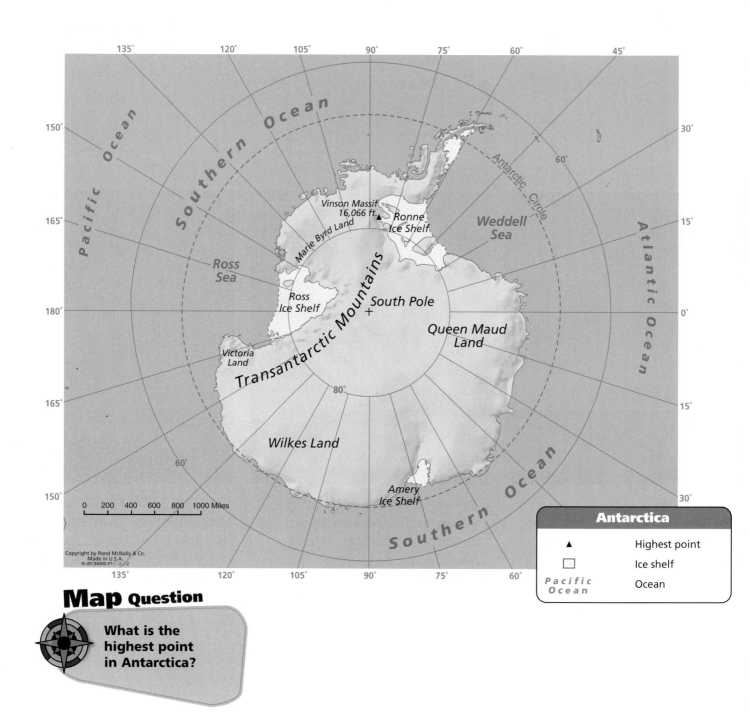

	Antarctica	
▲		Highest point
□		Ice shelf
Pacific Ocean		Ocean

Map Question

What is the highest point in Antarctica?

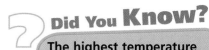

Lowest Recorded Temperature on Each Continent

Antarctica is the coldest place in the world.

Africa (-9°F) — Australia(-9°F)

South America (-27°F)

Europe (-67°F)

North America (-81°F)

Asia (-94°F)

Antarctica (-129°F)

Did You Know?

The highest temperature ever recorded in Antarctica is 59° F.

Emporer penguins

Emperor penguins live in large colonies on the sea ice along Antarctica's coast.

Antarctic iceberg

As temperatures get warmer in summer, pieces break off Antarctica's ice shelves. The pieces can form huge icebergs.

Scientists in Antarctica

Scientists study Antarctica during the summer. Very few people stay on this cold, barren continent during the winter.

Antarctica through History

About 200 years ago

Explorers first sighted Antarctica.

About 40 years ago

Twelve countries agreed to use Antarctica only for scientific research.

1700 → 1800 → 1900 → 2000

About 100 years ago

A Norwegian explorer reached the South Pole.

Geographical Terms

This drawing shows many features of the earth. To find the meanings of some of the terms, look in the word list below.

Canyon: A deep, narrow valley with high, steep sides

Cape: A narrow piece of land that extends into the sea

Coast: Land along a large lake, sea, or ocean

Desert: A large land area that receives little rainfall

Forest: A large land area covered with trees

Gulf: A large area of water within a curved coastline; a gulf is larger than a bay and smaller than a sea

Harbor: A protected body of water where ships can anchor safely

Hill: A small land area higher than the land around it

Island: A piece of land surrounded by water

Lake: An inland body of water

Mountain: Land that rises much higher than the land around it

Peninsula: A piece of land nearly surrounded by water

Plain: A large, flat land area

Plateau: A large, high land area that is generally flat

River: A body of fresh water that flows from higher to lower land

Sea: A large body of salt water partly surrounded by land

Valley: The lower land between hills or mountains

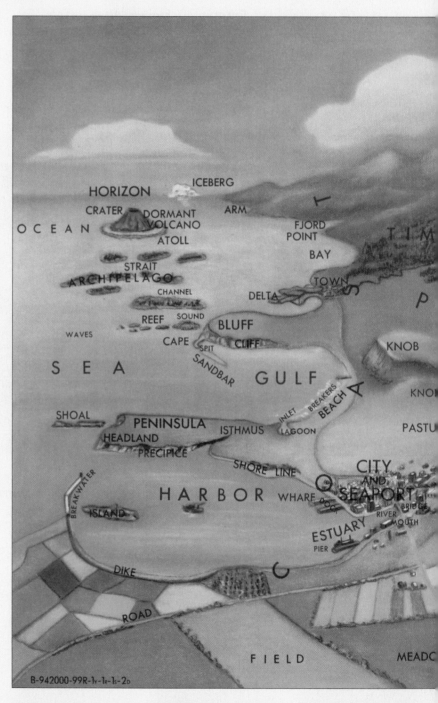

Coast

Desert

Forest

SUMMIT
GLACIER SNOWLINE
TIMBERLINE
PEAK
PASS
MOUNTAIN RANGE
FOOTHILLS
ACTIVE VOLCANO
CINDER CONE
CANYON
GULCH
HILL
TABLELAND
PLATEAU
BRINK
VILLAGE
DIVIDE
RESERVOIR
FOREST
VALLEY
STREAM
PIEDMONT
WATERFALL
CHASM
DAM
M
O
U
N
T
A
I
N
GROVE
BROOK
RAPIDS
TUNNEL
POWER PLANT
CANAL
IRRIGATED LAND
LAKE
MARSH
RIVER BAYOU BRANCH
LEVEE
RAILROAD
RIGHT BANK
LEFT BANK
WOODS
LOCKS
GORGE
S
L
O
P
E
R
I
D
G
E
OASIS
CULTIVATED LAND
CRAG
DUNE
MESA
AIRPORT
POND
LEDGE
DESERT
WAY

Harbor

Island

Mountain

Valley

North
America

Caribbean Sea

Atlantic
Ocean

Caracas

Venezuela

Orinoco River

Georgetown
Medellín
Paramaribo
Guyana
Bogota
Cayenne
Suriname
Colombia
French Guiana

Galapagos
Islands

Quito
Equator

Ecuador

Manaus
Belém

Amazon River

Amazon
Basin

Pacific

B r a z i l

Recife

Ocean

Lima
Peru

Brasília
Salvador

La Paz

Bolivia

Sucre

Paraguay

Chile

River

Rio de Janeiro

Asunción
São
Paulo

Tropic of Capricorn

N

Argentina
W E

Paraná

Cerro Aconcagua
22,831 ft.
S
Santiago

Uruguay

Buenos
Aires
Montevideo

Andes

Pampas

Atlantic

Ocean

Patagonia

Falkland
Islands
(United Kingdom)

Map Question

What symbol on
the map stands for
a river?

Cape Horn

0   200   400   600   800   1000 Miles

Copyright by Rand McNally & Co.
Made in U.S.A.
N-JRC40000-P1

Symbols

Symbols are lines, colors, and shapes that stand for something else. Maps use symbols to stand for real places on the earth.

Ocean

River

City

Mountains

Legend

A **map legend** explains what the symbols on a map mean.

	South America
———	Country boundary
⌢	River
▲	Highest point
Bolivia	Country
✪ Lima	Country capital
■ São Paulo	City
Atlantic Ocean	Ocean

Compass Rose

A **compass rose** shows directions on a map. The letters stand for **N**orth, **E**ast, **S**outh, and **W**est.

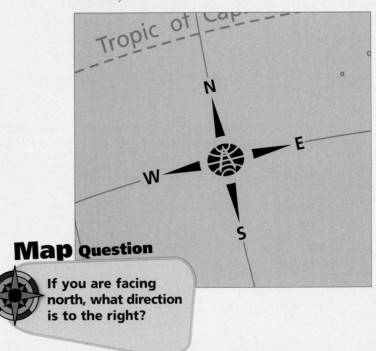

Tropic of Cap...

N
W — E
S

Map Question

If you are facing north, what direction is to the right?

Bar Scale

A **bar scale** helps you understand distances on a map.

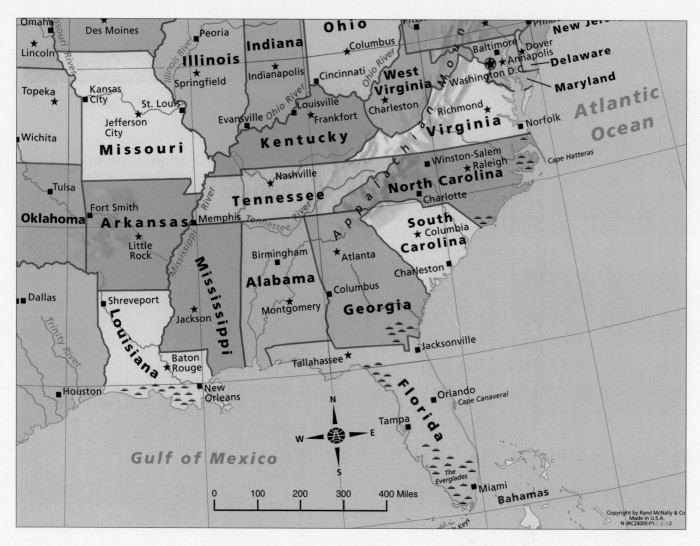

The bar scale on this map shows that one inch stands for about 225 miles on the earth.

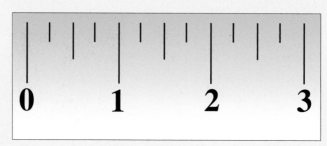

A bar scale helps you measure distances on a map.

Copy the bar scale onto a strip of paper.

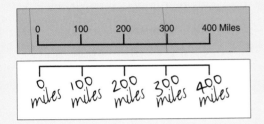

Use your paper bar scale to find distances on the map.

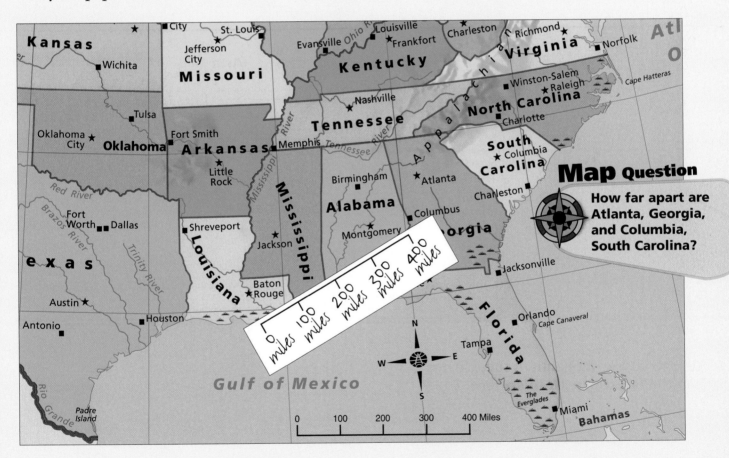

Baton Rouge, Louisiana, and Montgomery, Alabama, are a little more than 300 miles apart.

Latitude

Latitude lines run east and west on globes and maps.

The **equator** is a latitude line that divides the earth in half. It represents 0 degrees latitude. All other latitude lines are numbered based upon their distance from the equator.

Each half of the earth is called a **hemisphere**.

All land and water north of the equator is in the **Northern Hemisphere**.

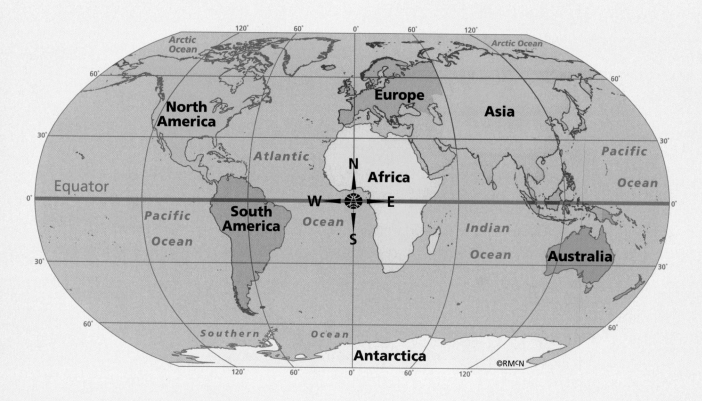

All land and water south of the equator is in the **Southern Hemisphere**.

Longitude

Longitude lines run north and south from pole to pole on globes and maps.

The **prime meridian** is the longitude line that represents 0 degrees of longitude.

All other longitude lines are numbered based upon their distance from the prime meridian.

Each half of the earth is called a **hemisphere**.

All land and water west of the prime meridian is in the **Western Hemisphere**.

All land and water east of the prime meridian is in the **Eastern Hemisphere**.

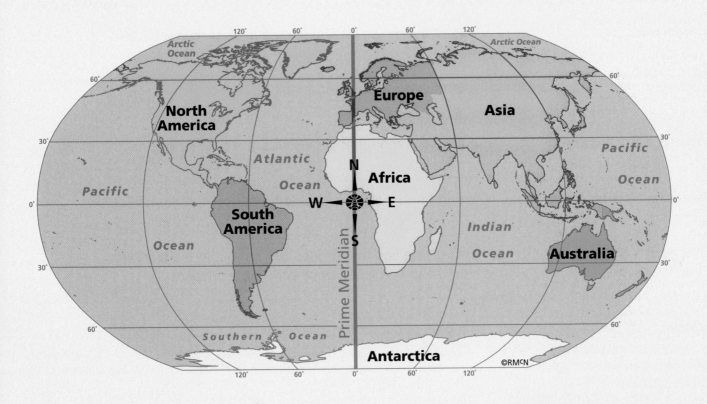

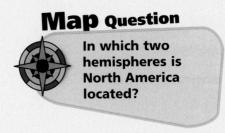

Map Question

In which two hemispheres is North America located?

Glossary

bar scale the part of a map that helps you measure distances; the bar scale tells how many miles on the earth's surface are shown by each inch on the map

climate how hot or cold, wet or dry a place is over a long period of time

compass rose the part of a map that shows directions; the letters on a compass rose stand for North, East, South, and West

continent one of the seven largest bodies of land on the earth

country a land that has a government

country boundary a line on a map that shows where a country begins and ends

Eastern Hemisphere all land and water on the earth east of the prime meridian

equator the latitude line that divides the earth into the Northern Hemisphere and the Southern Hemisphere

globe a model of the earth

hemisphere half of the earth

latitude lines lines that run east and west on a globe or a map

longitude lines lines that run north and south on a globe or a map

manufacturing making goods

map legend	the part of a map that explains what the symbols on the map mean
map	a drawing of the earth's surface
national capital	the city where a nation's government leaders work
Northern Hemisphere	all land and water on the earth north of the equator
ocean	one of the five largest bodies of salt water on the earth
prime meridian	the longitude line that divides the earth into the Eastern Hemisphere and the Western Hemisphere
regions	places that have something in common
Southern Hemisphere	all land and water on the earth south of the equator
sphere	a ball; the earth is shaped like a sphere
state	part of a country; the United States is a country with fifty states
state boundary	a line on a map that shows where a state begins and ends
state capital	a city where state government leaders work
symbols	lines, colors, and shapes that stand for something else
Western Hemisphere	all land and water on the earth west of the prime meridian

Index

Index Abbreviations